Dropshipping

The Complete Guide to Dropshipping (How to Create a Profitable Six Figure Online Business and Make Passive Income Without Having Your Own Inventory)

This document is geared towards providing exact and reliable information in regards to the topic and issue covered. The publication is sold with the idea that the publisher is not required to render accounting, officially permitted, or otherwise, qualified services. If advice is necessary, legal or professional, a practiced individual in the profession should be ordered.

- From a Declaration of Principles which was accepted and approved equally by a Committee of the American Bar Association and a Committee of Publishers and Associations.

The information provided herein is stated to be truthful and consistent, in that any liability, in terms of inattention or otherwise, by any usage or abuse of any policies, processes, or directions contained within is the solitary and utter responsibility of the recipient reader. Under no circumstances will any legal responsibility or blame be held against the publisher for any reparation, damages, or monetary loss due to the information herein, either directly or indirectly.

Respective authors own all copyrights not held by the publisher.

The information herein is offered for informational purposes solely, and is universal as so. The presentation of the information is without contract or any type of guarantee assurance.

The trademarks that are used are without any consent, and the publication of the trademark is without permission or backing by the trademark owner. All trademarks and brands within this book are for clarifying purposes only and are the owned by the owners themselves, not affiliated with this document.

Table of Contents

Introduction

Earning a passive income online gives you the unique and incredible opportunity to maximize your income and step into the blissful world of financial freedom. When you are able to produce a six-figure online business that requires little of your involvement for maintenance, you eliminate your need to stay in the struggle and grind of a 9-to-5 corporate job. You open up your window of opportunity and give yourself the chance to live a life that is free, effortless, and bountiful.

Dropshipping companies are an incredible way to tap into the online retail industry without having to spend a great deal of money to get started. They are one of the best opportunities for anyone to take advantage of as very little is required in order for you to get started. To start, you simply have to set up your website or use a hosting website, plug in some products from qualified dropshipping wholesaler suppliers, and start marketing your business! Through effective management strategies and strong marketing techniques you will inevitably establish a business that will earn you a major income, up to six-figures and beyond!

There are many valuable benefits that you can enjoy if you start a dropshipping company of your own. Some of these benefits include: low overhead and zero need to carry inventory, low startup costs, and convenient automation systems. This business opportunity is truly one of the best ones available to anyone who is seeking to make a major income from the online world of e-commerce. Regardless of where your launch point is, you can definitely create a business that will earn you a massive amount of income.

"*Dropshipping:* The Complete Guide to Dropshipping (How to Create a Profitable Six-Figure Online Business and Make Passive Income Without Having Your Own Inventory)" will guide you through absolutely everything you need to know in order to begin your own successful dropshipping business. You will learn about how you can begin your business, how you can manage your business, how to market your business, common mistakes to avoid, various tips and tricks to launch your business into success, and so much more. By the end of this book, you will have all of the skills and confidence that you need in order to cultivate your own business and earn a massive profit as a result. All you have to do is implement the simple-to-follow steps and watch your business grow!

If you are ready to release the caged lifestyle of a 9-to-5 job that requires excessive amounts of time and effort and start earning a passive income online, then you are ready to design your own dropshipping business. Each chapter has been specially designed to ensure you have all of the tools you need to succeed with your dropshipping business. As you read, be sure to complete the suggested activities so that you can maximize the success you experience with your business. Finally, please enjoy.

Chapter 1: Understanding Dropshipping

Many people in the online space are talking about dropshipping companies. The idea sounds amazing: you don't carry any inventory and you use a host website (or your own) to earn a major profit. Before you get started, however, it is important that you know as much as possible about what dropshipping is and how it works.

What Is Dropshipping?

Dropshipping is a method of retail fulfillment that takes the requirement of carrying inventory off of the store owner. In traditional stores, even online, retailers are required to carry inventory so that when a sale is made they can ship the product to the purchasing customer. With dropshipping, however, the sale is fulfilled by a warehouse that carries stock for the store owner. Dropshipping warehouses are typically third party companies that are responsible for supplying stock to several different companies.

Because of the setup of a dropshipping store, the merchant is never required to see, touch, or carry inventory for the purpose of business. At most, the merchant may purchase samples to ensure the quality of the products they are selling on their retail store.

How Does It Work?

When a merchant stocks their online store with dropshipping-supplied products, the store is set up identical to any other retail store. You can go on a host website (such as Shopify) or go to the merchant's own web hosted store, which will show off all of the products that are for sale. From there, you decide what you are seeking to purchase and then you put it in your cart. Once you check out, the merchant is paid, and then the merchant automatically pays the dropshipper for the product. The dropshipper then ships the product to the paying customer, and the chain is complete. Aside from hosting the actual sales, the merchant is not involved in any of the rest of the process.

Will I Actually Make a Profit?

Due to a lower startup cost, lower overhead, and the ease of setting up a website online, it is actually extremely simple to make a profit from dropshipping companies. You simply create a website, host sales, and get paid every time someone purchases products from your website. You can host as many or as few products as you desire, and you can set the prices to whatever your desired price range is. As a result, you have a large amount of control over how much you will profit from each sale.

What Else Do I Need to Know?

Dropshipping is one of the easiest online businesses to run. You are not required to do a significant amount of work in order to maintain your shop, which means it is a highly passive income stream. Despite this fact, there is still work you will need to put into hosting your website or sales and ensuring that they succeed. Throughout this book, you will learn how you can operate your dropshipping business for the highest benefit. You can either be highly involved or outsource everything and have minimal involvement in the process. Ideally, especially if you are just starting out, you will want to be more involved so that you gain maximum profit. As you grow, then you may consider outsourcing even more of the work.

Dropshipping is a sophisticated opportunity to host an online retail store. It makes shopping online easy for both the merchant and the customer. It is highly cost effective and can be accomplished by virtually anyone who desires to create an online business and start earning money from it. You are not required to have any special talents when it comes to hosting a dropshipping retail store and earning profits from it, you simply need a willingness to learn and a basic understanding of the internet.

Chapter 2: Pros and Cons of Dropshipping

Although dropshipping is a highly promising business opportunity, it is important to have a clear understanding of the pros and cons of dropshipping. This business venture is highly profitable and therefore it can be easy to forget that there are alternatives that you need to consider when you are getting started. In this chapter, we are going to honestly explore the different pros and cons associated with starting a dropshipping business online.

Cons

Let's start by getting right into it and identifying what the negative aspects of dropshipping are. That way, you are completely clear on what the drawbacks are that are associated with dropshipping.

Stock Shortages

When you are running an online retail business that is fulfilled by dropshippers, you run the potential of there being sudden stock shortages that will negatively affect your business. Stock shortages occur when several websites post that they carry an item and then the item sells out. As a result, you may end up having to refund your customers or request that they wait for back ordered items. Regardless, it can negatively affect your business and cut into your profits.

Since you do not have control over stock and have no foresight over stock quantities, it can be difficult for you to manage situations such as this. While those who carry their own inventory can identify when stock is running low and stock up, dropshippers can only do so much. Often, because of how many people are stocking their products it can be hard for the dropshipping company to know when they are going to need to restock their products. Additionally, there is often a situation where they require such large stock amounts to fulfill their own orders that it can take some time for items to come back into stock.

Higher Cost Per Item

Companies who stock their own items often save a large amount of money on items because they are purchasing such large quantities. These savings are often applied to wholesale or large orders of manufactured products because people are promising to purchase such a massive number of items that they are earning the wholesaler or manufacturer a large amount of money.

When you work with a dropshipping company, you are not purchasing massive quantities, therefore, you do not get the same savings that other manufacturers would. You are then required to pay an extra $2-$5 per item, which can be a little more expensive. However, you might also consider that you are not running the risk of purchasing excessive stock, therefore you will save money in other ways.

Unable to Provide Custom Photographs or Information

There are many circumstances where customers want to purchase something from you but may request further information about products you are selling. Since you do not have direct interaction with the product, it can be hard for you to provide further assistance to these customers. While you may be able to learn more about the product to tell the customer, you will not be able to provide certain details promptly, nor will you be able to provide custom photographs of the products for the inquiring customer. For some customers, this may lead to them purchasing elsewhere or not purchasing at all because they do not have enough knowledge about the product in order to make the purchase.

You Get Blame for Supplier Problems

If you pick high-quality suppliers, you likely won't have to worry about dealing with this often. However, there are circumstances where a supplier might slip up or the quality of a product may not be what the customer expected and therefore you must take the blame. The most you can do at this point is relay the information back to your supplier and do your best to rectify the situation with your unhappy customer. Because you do not have direct control over the product, it may be difficult for you to really do anything about the situation in order to truly make a difference.

These are the largest cons that are present in the dropshipping industry. You will likely experience some of your own, however, these are the most prominent ones that you need to know about. Even though these are cons that can be associated with the business, there are certain actions you can take to reduce the risk of you experiencing them and them having a negative effect on your business.

Pros

There are many pros associated with dropshipping businesses that can make them a highly promising business for virtually anyone who is wanting to get into online retailing. The following list will highlight the best benefits you can expect when you are working with a dropshipping business.

Passive Income

When you start a dropshipping business, you ultimately establish an online retailer store that provides you with passive income. Due to how easy it is to run an online dropshipping business, you do not need to do a significant amount of work to keep the business running smoothly. As a result, you end up earning an incredible income for very little.

Passive income streams are an incredible opportunity for you to scale your income because there is little that you are required to do to earn that income stream. As a result, you can invest slightly more into building that business, you can invest your time and efforts into an alternative income source, or you can do both.

Easy to Grow

When you run a dropshipping business, it is extremely easy to grow your business to any size you want. You may want to start as a boutique business, but it is extremely simple to expand the amount of business you run through your website. Simply increase the amount of traffic you receive and then add more dropship items to your store. As a result, your business will grow and you will be able to infinitely expand. The only two things you need in order to grow are effective marketing strategies and the time to add new products to your store on a regular basis.

Due to the minimal investment it takes in order to scale your business, it can be extremely easy to grow it as large as you want. Whether you want to carry tens, hundreds, or even thousands of products, it is completely up to you. The more products you stock, however, the more you may want to consider hiring an assistant to help you look over the entire store and make sure that all of your product sale pages and descriptions are set up correctly.

Lifetime Value for Customers

Customers appreciate building a relationship with a company that they can shop from on an ongoing basis. Customers want to be able to return to your store for years to come in order to purchase from you, especially once they discover that you are reliable, have high-quality items, and are excellent with providing customer service.

When you run a dropshipping business, it is easy for you to add products to your virtual shelves that will continue to please your customers. After you identify exactly what your customers like and prefer, you can continue stocking those types of items by building sales pages for them. This will keep people returning to your page, keep them spending money, and further increase their trust in you and your business.

Low Startup Cost

Starting up a dropshipping business is extremely simple and rather cost-effective. If you have skills with building a website, then you simply pay the hosting fees and any other fees associated with actually opening a business in your municipality, region, or country. There is virtually no cost associated with products and inventory themselves, therefore you do not have to worry about investing a significant amount of money into your startup. This means that nearly anyone can start a dropshipping business without the need to worry about taking out expensive business loans or stocking up on expensive inventory levels.

Low Overhead

Just like it is inexpensive to start your dropshipping business, it is also inexpensive to maintain it. Aside from paying for service fees, it is simple for you to keep everything running. With a business where you are responsible for stocking inventory, it can become costly. If any simple thing needs to be changed in the supply chain, you can run into high expenses that can lead to you spending a large amount of money towards the change. It may also result in you having entire shipments of products that are not the quality you were looking for and therefore you have money that is unrecoverable.

In a dropshipping business, you can easily discontinue items or change the items you are providing. Since you are not directly involved in the supply chain, there are very little costs associated with it for you and you do not run the risk of incurring major losses as a result. Ultimately, it is extremely cheap for you to keep your business running. The primary thing you need to focus on is keeping your site and products updated. Aside from that, everything else is self-maintaining.

Expand into Any Market

Being in the online marketplace means that you can expand into virtually any market. Dropshippers can generally send their products to nearly anywhere on the globe, therefore you do not have to worry about where you are sending your products because anyone can purchase them. This means that you can tap into the unlimited supply of the worldwide market and push your business as far as you desire. There are no limits on how much you can grow your business or how far you can ship your items.

Unlimited Inventory

Working with dropshippers means that you have access to unlimited inventory. Since dropshippers are often servicing several companies, they tend to carry large amounts of stock to satisfy customers. When they begin to run out of items, they will restock them and therefore you gain access to more stock. You are not required to keep anything in stock or save money out of your profits to restock items when they begin running low. Instead, that is all looked after by the dropshipping company. It makes it extremely simple and cost effective for you, as there is virtually nothing needed by you in order to keep your stock.

The Verdict

As with anything, there are positives and negatives associated with dropshipping. Although the negatives can be frustrating, they are rarely costly or highly negative for you and your business. It is extremely easy to use effective strategies to ensure that your company maintains a positive reputation and that your sales continue to expand.

There are many positive attributes associated with beginning your own dropshipping business. The benefits include very low risk, low startup and management fees, ease of growing business, and access to a passive income stream. There are many other benefits to the business as well, which you will gain access to when you start your own business.

When considered against other businesses, dropshipping has very minimal risks and few cons associated with it. It is one of the easiest businesses to get into, as well as one of the easiest businesses to get out of if it does not work for you, which you will learn about in a later chapter. If you have experience with a computer and with using the internet, then you have all of the skills you need to start your own dropshipping business. From there, all you have to do is learn the steps and apply them. Then, you will have your own successful dropshipping business earning you a massive six-figure passive income stream.

Chapter 3: The Basics of Getting Started

You've learned all about this promising business model and how it can earn you large money, and you are ready to get started. By now, you are likely convinced that the dropshipping business is an incredible business model for you to get into if you are seeking to tap into the online market and earn a large profit. So, we are going to explore the steps you need to take in order to successfully start your own dropshipping business!

Pick Your Niche

Before you even get into the process of building your business, you need to decide what you are going to sell. While some websites like Amazon.com can get away with selling virtually everything, people who are just starting out are better off if they stick to a single niche. Picking a niche gives you the opportunity to identify exactly who your target audience is, and then successfully market towards that audience. While you can expand in the future, you want to start with something smaller and manageable.

There are a few things that go into making a niche that is going to be a success for your business. First, you want to pick a niche that is performing well. It should not be saturated, but it should be big enough that you actually have the potential to earn a profit from it. Just because a niche is a niche doesn't mean it is a good one. In addition to a niche that performs well, you also want to pick one that you are actually interested in. If you are interested in the niche you are getting involved with, you will have significantly higher success with your business than if you are not interested in it at all. Being interested in the niche you are going to sell in gives you the advantage of having the opportunity to understand what your target audience wants and how you can meet their needs.

To start the process of picking your niche, start by writing down about 5-10 categories for things that you are actually interested in and would enjoy selling. From those categories, you can start conducting your research. Find out which ones perform well and which ones don't. Take the ones that do and use these as the basis for further research. Start by going to places like Shopify and Amazon and looking at how these categories perform. Furthermore, take note of who is in the industry already selling products. To be successful in a niche, regardless of how many people are currently selling in it, you need to be able to have a competitive edge. Identifying whether or not you will have a competitive edge will come from doing some research about suppliers. While you certainly don't need to pick one yet, you will want to discover what type of pricing you are going to be offering for various items in each niche. Find one where you can offer comparable and competitive pricing.

Once you have conducted your research, you will likely have one or two niches left that are qualified for a successful business. If you have one, then your choice is clear. However, if you end up with two or three, then you are going to have to decide which one you want to do. If the choice isn't obvious based on niche performance, then you can simply choose which one you would enjoy most. The final answer will be the niche that you are going to build your entire business around.

Identify Your Ideal Market

Assuming you have chosen a niche that you are actually interested in, you should have a simple time identifying who your target audience is. Knowing who your target audience is will set you up for the future of your business. Every decision you make will be based on the intention of serving this audience and creating a brand and business that will meet their needs and attract their interest. If you cannot effectively communicate with your target audience, then you are not going to be able to make any sales.

It may seem easier to create a broader audience so that you have more potential reach, but the reality is that this will actually dampen your efforts. In the beginning, you want to be very specific about who your target audience is. Once you have successfully served them, it is likely that others will develop an interest in your business and you will be able to broaden your audience. However, keep that as an opportunity for future growth and remain clear and focused on one specific ideal consumer for the time being.

When you are preparing to outline your ideal market, start by researching similar companies and who they are targeting. Take notice of exactly who they are focusing on in their ads. Is it families? Single females? Single males? Pre-marital couples? Individuals with specific interests? Get as clear on the exact person that is being targeted as you possibly can. You can also conduct some research by looking into the products themselves. See if you can find the products being discussed on forums anywhere and take note of the type of people who are engaging in the conversation the most. These are the exact people you are going to want to identify as your ideal audience.

The following list consists of things you should consider when you are targeting customers in your business. If you can answer these questions, then you should be clear on who you are targeting which will make establishing your business significantly easier:

1. What is the age range of your targeted audience?
2. Is there a primary gender that appears to be interested in your niche?
3. What hobbies do these people have?
4. Are there any specific phrases or slang that they use when speaking about this niche?
5. How does this particular product category serve their needs?
6. Why are they interested in these products?
7. Do they have anything else in common, regardless of whether or not it pertains directly to the niche?
8. Is there any particular icon, color, logo, or "style" that they tend to be drawn towards?
9. What are their current favorite brands? Who are they purchasing products like yours from the most?
10. What "feeling" do you get from these people?

When you answer these questions, you make it significantly easier for you to develop your brand. You also make the process of choosing products and marketing easier as well. It is vital that you establish the answers to these questions now as opposed to later. Answering them now can be the defining factor that sets you up for total success in your business overall. It is absolutely vital that you take the time to answer these questions in as much detail as possible. While it can take a bit longer than you may have anticipated, it can add a tremendous amount of value to your ability to create a sustainable and successful business out of the gate.

Outline a Brand That Serves Your Ideal Market

Now is the first time that you are going to put your market research to good use. When you are building your website and marketing your new business, you are going to want to have a specific brand image that you operate under. The market research you have conducted is going to assist you in deciding exactly how you are going to create your brand, what image you are going to portray, and how you should portray it in order to speak to your ideal client. If you are already knowledgeable in your niche and have some level of passion in it, then this should be fairly easy for you. The market research you have conducted should make it even easier.

There is a great deal of detail that goes into creating a brand. You want to make sure that your image is consistent, your vocabulary and language should be consistent, and the "personality" your company gives off should be consistent. Should you ever hire anyone to help you, they should be able to create content for your brand that is consistent with the image that you have created. This way, people will be able to identify your brand and establish a relationship with your business as they will feel a sense of recognition and trust for the brand you have created.

The first step you should take when creating your brand is considering your image. Your image is created using actual images, colors, and specific designs. Your primary opportunity to create your image is on your website, though you can use social media profiles to emphasize your image as well. In fact, if you have any social media profiles they should all utilize your brand image to create the consistency that is required to have a strong brand. All of your marketing and ad campaigns should maintain this image as well. Before you start structuring your website and other major projects, start by sitting down and identifying what you want your brand to be. Websites like

Pinterest are excellent for choosing brand designs as they offer a series of color palettes and fonts that flow well together. In addition to colors and fonts, you will want to consider actual images. Most brands have a specific symbol that goes along with their brand, such as Nike's check mark or apple's computer. You should choose a symbol that will be used across your brand as well. Then, you should also choose specific images. If you are selling yoga products, for example, you may wish to use only images that reflect the outdoors, freedom, and holistic wellness primarily through yoga poses and other similar activities.

Once you have created your brand image, you should carry on to create your brand's vocabulary and "personality". Using the catch phrases and vocabulary you identified during your market research process, you should develop a slogan. You should also practice creating content and copy that uses this slang and phrasing in order to effectively communicate with your targeted audience. Whenever you are posting about your business, you should use this vocabulary and personality-type in order to communicate with your audience.

Creating a solid brand is vital to the success of your business. In order to have a business that thrives, you need to be able to create a brand that is identifiable and strong. Believe it or not, your brand is a large part of your marketing. If you are able to create a brand that is identifiable, people are going to think about you a lot more frequently. Consider the Apple logo, for example. Whenever someone sees the Apple logo, even if there are no identifiable phrases surrounding the logo, they are well aware of what the logo stands for. The brand has identified itself so successfully that in many cases people even say "Apple" or when they look at an apple they may subconsciously think of the brand itself. This type of branding provides you with the opportunity to stay relevant and fresh in people's minds. While you will not have this immediately, you should aim for this right from the beginning. Thinking about your future success now is what will set you up to earn a six-figure income through your dropshipping business.

Choose Your Platform

Since you are planning on establishing an online retail business, you want to make sure that you have an effective platform to run off of. Think of your platform as your store front: you want one that will successfully reflect your business and your brand. It should be clean, crisp, easy for users to interact with, and easy for you to interact with as well. Everything should be streamlined so that the shopping experience is simple and effective. If it becomes too difficult, the layout is too sloppy, or the website is confusing, people will be less likely to purchase from your website.

The primary areas you want to focus on with your website include clean and crisp product pages, easy ability to submit and collect payments, easy ability for customer to access support, and an effective backend management system that enables you to operate the website easily. Your website is the driving force for your entire business, so it is important that both you and your customer have an easy time using it as this is what will increase the success of your business.

It may seem like a big task to have to build your website, but it truly is not that difficult. If you absolutely do not want to do it, there are many professional website builders you can hire to complete the task for you. Remember, however, hiring one of these website designers will cost you a fair amount of money, especially since you want to hire one who will be able to create a highly professional website which will positively reflect your business.

If you do not want to host an independent website for your dropshipping business, you can always choose a platform to run your business from. Shopify, Amazon, WooCommerce, and BigCommerce are all websites you can use to host your dropshipping business. It is recommended that you go with a host that has high traffic if you are going to choose a third party platform for your business as this will increase your amount of potential traffic which will increase the number of sales you gain.

In Conclusion

The earliest stages of establishing your business are the most sensitive. You want to make sure that you launch a business that will be as successful as possible from the start. The more effort you put into establishing a successful business now, the more success you will experience later. It also leads to having less work to do later as you have laid a strong foundation now for your business.

Market research is vital in the early stages as this is what will give you the best opportunity to leverage your business and establish one that can adequately serve the needs and desires of your targeted market. If you fail to conduct market research in the early stages, you may end up designing an entire business that fails to effectively communicate with your targeted audience. Then, regardless of the quality of your products, website, or service, you will likely never gain customers. It is absolutely critical that you develop a strong brand with an effective ability to communicate with your target audience early on. This will give you the highest opportunity to succeed in your business on a long-term basis.

Chapter 4: Finding Suppliers

Aside from having a strong website and brand image, you also need to have great suppliers when you are running a dropshipping business. Since dropshipping has become such a popular business model the number of suppliers has increased exponentially. As a new dropshipping business owner this means that you have a higher selection of suppliers to choose from, giving you the opportunity to choose the best ones for your clients.

Finding and choosing suppliers can be somewhat of a daunting process. There is a lot that goes into identifying a qualified supplier and choosing to host their products on your website. Many suppliers seek to provide high-quality products as this is what keeps them in business, but it doesn't mean that every supplier will maintain these high standards. It is imperative that you research your suppliers and ensure that you are choosing the best ones in order to make sure that your business is providing the best quality of products possible. If your products are not high quality, your customers will likely be disappointed and therefore the word-of-mouth regarding your business will be poor. In business, especially in the beginning, social proof (word-of-mouth advertising) can make or break you.

Understanding Dropshipping Suppliers

Dropshipping suppliers are a unique type of wholesaler that carries stock and ships it directly to your client. When you work together with a dropshipper, you create an agreement that you will advertise their product on your website and whenever someone purchases the product through you, you will then purchase that product through the wholesaler and they will ship it to your client. Instead of purchasing several products at once and keeping an inventory, the dropshipping wholesaler keeps the inventory and takes over all inventory-related tasks associated with your business.

It is important to understand that not all dropshipping wholesalers are created equally. There are many retail stores that pretend to be wholesale suppliers when in all reality they are actually simply taking their piece of the pie in the supply chain. A true wholesaler is a company who purchases their products directly from a manufacturer. If the supplier is purchasing them from an alternative wholesaler, they are simply a discounted retail store and not a true wholesaler. You want to avoid these stores as they can impose a significant amount of trouble and risk for your business. For example, if there is a quality issue there is often little to nothing that these wholesalers can do about it. However, if you were to discuss the issue with a true wholesaler they would be able to communicate with their manufacturer and rectify the situation going forward. Additionally, true wholesalers offer significantly better pricing deals on their products than retail stores attempting to be wholesalers as they do not have to impose a secondary price increase in order to get their slice of the profit. It essentially eliminates a potentially highly costly tier.

Dropshipping wholesalers are an important part of your business as they provide the products for your clients. It is vital that you choose a wholesaler who is trustworthy, quality-oriented, and capable of providing you with the best pricing possible. Make sure that you choose a true wholesaler and not a retailer imposing as a wholesaler.

Buyer Beware

It is important to understand that there are a lot of "fake" wholesalers on the market who are trying to get their slice of profit from the dropshipping business. If you want to maximize your profit and minimize your expenses, you need to identify who these are and weed them out of your potential wholesaler list.

Something to understand is that legitimate wholesalers are typically poor with their marketing strategies and therefore can be more difficult to discover. If a company does a great deal of marketing, there is a good chance that they are one of the retail-based "wholesalers" which you want to avoid.

Some ways that you can identify fake retail-based wholesalers include:

- Membership Fees: true wholesalers do not charge their customers monthly membership fees so that they can maintain their wholesaler status. If your potential supplier is asking for monthly membership fees, they are likely a fake company. *Note:* supplier directories (not actual suppliers) do tend to charge monthly membership fees. In this case, it is normal and is not typically proof that the directory itself is illegitimate.

- Public Sales: wholesalers do not sell to the public. They require you to create an actual wholesale account which means you have to provide them with proof of being a legitimate business and you will have to wait for your account to be approved. Then, you can begin purchasing their products at wholesale prices.
- Per-Order Fees: many wholesalers, legitimate included, have per-order fees. If you notice there is a per-order fee that ranges from $2 to $5 or more, you should note that this is a standard practice in the industry and it is not a sign that you are working with an illegitimate wholesaler.
- Minimum Order Sizes: many dropshipping companies run into difficulty with minimum order sizes. There are several wholesaler companies that require you to order a minimum order quantity for your initial order to prove that you are truly looking to do business and that you are not just window shopping. This can create an issue for dropshippers as the intention is that you do not have to carry stock. This is standard and does not signify that you are working with an illegitimate wholesaler. Some wholesalers will allow you to provide them with a credit value on your account where you don't actually have to receive stock but rather your initial orders are already covered by the credit you provided.

How to Locate Suppliers

Once you are clear on what is normal for wholesalers and what can signify an illegitimate wholesaler, you are ready to start actually seeking out suppliers for your business. This is where your part of the job becomes fun because you now get to shop around and decide what you want to stock your store with. There are many different strategies you can use to discover wholesalers and identify the ones that you want to work with.

Contacting manufacturers is an excellent way to find wholesalers for your business. When you contact the manufacturer, you can request a list of wholesalers who stock their products and then contact the wholesalers. This way you know that the wholesalers are working directly with the manufacturer and that they are not third-party retailers who are seeking to gain profit from your business. Once you have discovered who the wholesalers are you can begin contacting them and learning which wholesalers support dropshipping businesses. If they do, inquire about setting up an account with them. Most wholesalers carry a variety of stock from their manufacturers so these accounts will provide you with access to a number of different products from each manufacturer which is highly beneficial when you are creating your business. The less wholesale suppliers you are working with the easier it will be to keep your business organized.

Search engines provide an excellent opportunity to discover new wholesalers. However, you want to make sure that you are doing a significant amount of research with your wholesalers to ensure that you are working with legitimate suppliers. Make sure that you seek external reviewers for their company. Also, refrain from judging wholesalers based on their website. Those who are legitimate often have poorly constructed websites, so in many cases, the best suppliers are those who have outdated websites that look like they are straight out of the '90s. Additionally, simply searching "(product) wholesaler" may not be sufficient when you are using a search engine to locate suppliers. More often than not, their websites do not utilize SEO strategies, so you will have to use more modifiers to identify these companies. Try using words such as "distributor", "bulk", "supplier", "wholesaler" or "reseller".

Another wonderful tool when you are in the world of dropshipping is directories. Directory databases are excellent tools for people in the industry as they provide you with access to a list of suppliers based on your chosen market, niche, or product. The majority of directories, especially those you pay for, have a screening process in place to weed out illegitimate wholesalers, which can make your job a lot easier in the long run. Directories are excellent for quickly locating suppliers, but it is important to note that they are not necessary. You can locate wholesalers in alternative methods that are more cost-effective. Still, if you prefer the convenience and ease of a directory, you may find it worth it to invest in a membership so that you can access the comprehensive guide quickly. Make sure that you research the directory before investing in it so that you invest in one that will provide you with the highest value.

Contacting Suppliers

After you have located a series of potential suppliers, you are going to want to contact them. Ideally, you should contact between 5 and 10 suppliers as this will give you the opportunity to shop around and find the suppliers who can offer you the best value for your business. You may end up choosing more than one supplier which is completely normal and totally fine. With a dropshipping business, you want to have access to a significant number of products which may require you to have relationships with more than one supplier. Keep an open mind and prepare to build relationships with at least two suppliers in the beginning.

When you are contacting the suppliers you want to gain as much information about their business as possible. Ask them about whether or not they work with dropshippers, and if they do ask them how it looks from their end. The following questions are valuable questions to ask when you are getting to know your potential suppliers:

- Are there any minimum order quantities for initial purchases?
- Do they sell their products to the general public, or only to approved businesses?
- Are they willing to conduct business with a first-time business owner?
- Are there any monthly subscription fees associated with their business?
- What are their policies for returns?
- What is the type of data feed integration that is provided from the supplier?
- How long does it take for them to process an order on average?
- What fees are involved with the dropshipping process? Are there any "hidden" or additional fees?
- Who should you call if you have any questions or experience a problem with the dropshipper?

If any more questions come to mind, always feel free to ask. It is better to educate yourself as much as possible than it is to have unanswered questions and be left guessing. Since dropshipping suppliers are such a vital part of your business, you want to be sure that you are working with ones who will be able to serve you and your clients with high standards.

With the information you gather from each supplier, you should create a column list. Put the questions at the top, the supplier names down the side, and their answers through the spreadsheet. That way you can easily compare the suppliers and decide which two or three you are going to work with in the beginning. If you want to stay modest, you can work with one to start. However, you should keep an additional one or two on the back burner that you can contact when you are ready to expand your business and offer more products to your clients.

Once you have chosen which suppliers you want to work with, you should go ahead and contact those suppliers so that you can create your wholesale account with them. Keep in mind that this may take a while so you will want to start this sooner rather than later. You can always create an account and then keep it inactive for a short period of time, however, you do not want to have everything ready to go but still be waiting on the approval of your accounts.

Hosting Dropshipping Products

How you host your dropshipping products will depend on what platform you are using and who your suppliers are. Most suppliers have data integration systems that you simply plug into your dropshipping website and from there sales are made. You may or may not have to include your own product descriptions and create content and copy for the sales page. However, beyond that everything is typically managed by the data integration system. It should be fairly simple for you as the website host to keep everything streamlined and simple for your clients.

Maintaining the Relationship with Your Suppliers

While there isn't a lot that is needed to maintain a relationship with your wholesale suppliers, you do want to ensure that some level of relationship is maintained. You should spend time reaching out to your suppliers on a fairly regular basis to ensure that you have a positive relationship with them. Additionally, make sure that you pay attention to their requests. If they have special requests regarding orders, contacting them, or paying them, you should pay attention to these requests and carry them out in the desired method. This creates a positive interaction between you and the wholesaler which makes them much more likely to prefer you as a customer.

It is important also to always pay on time. You should never leave your wholesaler waiting for money. If you do, they may refuse to work with you on an ongoing basis. Remember, they are in business too, which requires them to make money in order to stay in business. You need to honor and respect their needs and treat them the way you would want your own clients to treat you in business.

Another thing to consider is that you are not the only one they are working with. Things may take time, including communications and order fulfillment. You need to be patient and allow for them to conduct their business. Since you are their client and they rely on you for their business, they are likely doing the best they can to ensure that your service experience is high quality. They are also doing the same for all of the other retailers they work with. Be sure that you are patient and that you respect that they have several other clients they are working with and therefore you will not always be at the top of their list.

When something goes wrong, which it will, it is important that you do not play the blame game with your suppliers. Accept that mistakes happen and move on with it in the most positive way possible. Of course, suppliers that are frequently experiencing problems that negatively affect your business should likely be phased out from your own business, but the occasional problem should not spark any large dispute between you and your supplier. Take the time to realize that their workers are only human and mistakes may take place. Work the situation out in a way that is positive for both yourself and your supplier and make sure that you are always kind and considerate when these situations arise. And remember, they *will* arise. Problems and unexpected situations always come up in business, the best way to prepare is to expect them to arise and be grateful when they don't.

Chapter 5: Automation

One of the best parts of having a dropshipping business is that you can integrate automation systems into your business. When your business is automated, it means that you are required to have even less involvement in the business than you initially needed to. With dropshipping already being a fairly passive business, turning it into an automated dropshipping business means that you will be required to put forth even less effort. Your business will be almost entirely passive and yet you will still be able to rapidly expand your income to assist you with creating a six-figure business.

There are many parts of your dropshipping business that can be automated, beyond the process of automating the shipments themselves. Automating these parts of your business will make running it even easier. The easier your business is to run, the greater opportunity you have to generate higher levels of revenue and profits from your business.

Forwarding Sales Orders

In a dropshipping business, you are not responsible for order fulfillment, but you are responsible for forwarding all orders you receive to your supplier so that they can fulfill orders for you. Doing this manually is not only tedious but can also generate bottlenecks and setbacks in your business. You also run into the potential that orders are not forwarded fast enough, so inventory levels run too low to fulfill your orders. It slows down the fulfillment process and overall it makes your job a lot more involved than you likely want it to be.

Automating this part of your business entails downloading software that automatically exports sales orders to your suppliers. As soon as an order is received in your marketplace or shopping cart, it will be forwarded to your supplier and they will be able to then fulfill the order. Each supplier will accept a different format of order, either through SFTP (SSH File Transfer Protocol), ETP (Exchange-traded products), or through CSV (Comma-Separated Values). Your supplier will let you know which format works, and from there you can choose a software that can assist you with completing the automation system.

Managing Inventory Levels

With any retailer, it is important that you manage inventory levels effectively. Since you are operating a dropshipping business where you have no interaction with the inventory of items you are selling, this can be slightly trickier. While many suppliers have systems in place that can provide you with this information to plug into your own website, some do not. Having this system automated can save you from having your process slow down when your supplier potentially runs out of stock or has to order a new shipment.

Automating your business using software that allows you to manage inventory levels effortlessly is extremely helpful but also important. It prevents you from having to inform your customers of setbacks, back orders, or provide refunds to those who are not willing to wait.

Prioritizing Suppliers

As a dropshipper, you will likely end up working with many different suppliers in order to stock your online retail shop with as many items as you would like to host. When you work with more shippers, however, it can become difficult to manage all of your suppliers by hand. Having an automated process where your computer prioritizes your suppliers for you can make scaling your business significantly easier. Instead of manually having to prioritize orders, you can rely on your computer to do it for you.

By using an automated prioritizing system, your computer will automatically route orders to suppliers. If one supplier is out of stock, the computer will reroute the item to an alternative supplier that is currently carrying stock. As a result, you will be able to scale your business as large or small as you desire and will not have to worry about your suppliers being out of stock. It also keeps you from having to manually prioritize suppliers and discover which ones are carrying stock for the items that you need.

Automating your dropshipping business makes it extremely easy for you to manage your entire business. Instead of having to focus on tedious tasks within' your business, you can focus on actually expanding your business instead. When you have these tasks automated, you can place your focus on adding products to your website, expanding your supplier list, and launching marketing campaigns to increase your sales traffic. Ultimately, you can invest more time in growth and less time in managing what you have already built.

Chapter 6: Growth Strategies

Aside from automating your business, you need to have strong growth strategies in place if you want to scale your business to be a six-figure earner. Having a successful growth strategy in place will allow you to know where you need to go with your business in order to be able to grow it to the level that you desire to grow it to. Strategies are everything. Consider your growth strategy a major part of your business plan. If you want your business to be successful, you need to have an adequate growth strategy in place.

This chapter is going to walk you through a specific growth strategy that will help ensure that you can push your business to become a six-figure income earner. If you follow each of the steps in this chapter, you will be able to build your business up to earn a massive income and serve you as a passive income stream for a long time to come.

Focus On Being Seen

Especially when you are initially starting out, you want to focus on being seen by the people you are targeting. While there are many different marketing strategies out there, you want to focus on the ones that are going to get you the highest visibility. While others may be nice and can be added later on, you want to emphasize your focus on the tactics that are going to earn you a high number of viewers and followers.

Social media, paid advertising, and influencers are the best opportunities for you to get your company seen. By emphasizing on these primary areas that are going to get you the most traction, you can increase the number of followers you get without overextending yourself into areas that are unnecessary right now. E-mail lists are important too, but you don't need one right away. You can start establishing that when you begin making sales from your website. This will be the next place you want to expand into, however. Everything else can wait until you have enough business moving in order to implement the strategies. You may even decide to wait until you can hire an assistant to help cover all of the marketing tasks.

With social media, you can create brand-specific profiles and use them as an opportunity to communicate with your customers. Regular status updates through sharing interesting and informative content and sharing entertaining content can really help increase the amount of engagement you gain from your followers. As a result, they will become more interested in your website and what you are selling. Make sure that everything you share on your social media platform follows your brand image and reputation, as well as makes clear sense. It should drive customers to either want to read more of the content you've shared *or* directly to your website so that they can make a purchase.

Paid advertising is an excellent opportunity to reach new leads. You can use social media accounts as a basis for launching paid advertising, which makes your social media accounts extra useful. Your paid advertisements will be pushed to reach more people than your simple posts will be, so you can feel confident that you will reach the eyes of more people and therefore you will have a greater impact on the amount of traction your content will have. If you do not want to use social media for paid advertisements, or if you want to take it a step further, Google Adwords and Amazon both have excellent paid advertising opportunities that can increase the amount of visibility you get with potential leads.

Influencers are one of the best opportunities to get in front of a new audience and develop a rapport with them effortlessly. When you send your product to an influencer, they talk about it to their audience. Since the influencer already has trust with their audience, you get the element of social proof and social approval added into this marketing platform. Instead of having to rely on a single advertisement to attract people, gain their trust, and encourage a sale, you can use an influencer who already has the trust of their audience. Once the audience sees how much the influencer likes your product(s) they will be much more likely to actually purchase from you. Additionally, if someone sees your advertisements and searches your company to learn more about your quality, they may stumble upon these influencers and gain valuable information about how much they liked your product. Using influencers as a marketing opportunity is an excellent way to increase your sales. It is highly recommended that you consider this avenue and use it throughout your dropshipping business career.

Stay Simple

The more your business grows, the more you may be drawn into taking on difficult tasks in order to keep your business sophisticated and ahead of the curve. The reality is that if you make your job any harder than it needs to be, your business will fail. You need to always be sure that you are implementing simple strategies that can be easily managed for the interest of your business. Automated emailing systems, other forms of automation, sticking to one or two areas of marketing and customer engagement, and staying as simple as possible with your brand image are all important parts of keeping your business easy to manage and keeping the income stream passive.

Many people get the idea that as their business grows they can begin implementing more complex strategies in order to further business growth. The reality is that the steps that got you to where you are now can get you significantly further if you continue to implement them. Stay simple, stay focused, and specialize in a few areas instead of trying to specialize in the whole thing. You will notice that this has a more positive impact on your growth than turning to complex strategies does. This is not simply about keeping your income stream passive, it is about keeping your income stream active as well.

Let Your Competition Do the Work

One of the best things you can do as a business owner is keeping an eye on your competition and let them do the work for you. Many new business owners want to try and stay edgy and ahead of the game by introducing new and exciting products to their virtual shelves. This can end up in you introducing many items that simply don't have any impact on your clients. Instead of playing the hit-or-miss game, let your competition do the work for you.

Keep a close eye on your competition and watch what products they are selling. When a particular product, category, or product line appears to be performing well, then you can jump in and add this to your own business. Take some time to review the feedback that company has been getting and use that as an opportunity to offer even better products in your store, and market these highlights. For example, if your competition is selling a unique pen and you notice several reviews that say the grip is not soft enough, you can stock your store with a pen that has an extremely soft comfort grip. Then, you can market that feature and target the audience that has been working with your competitor. This will show them that you have the better product because you are offering the types of products that directly serve their needs and satisfy any complaints they may have with the competition.

It is a rookie mistake to try and stay ahead of your competition by ignoring them. The irony of business is that the easiest way to stay ahead of your competition is to sit back about one to two steps and let them lead the way. Then, you can use their market research, experience, and consumer feedback to create a better plan for your own business and capitalize on their learning experiences. It saves you money and time while also giving you an excellent growth strategy that can scale your business rapidly.

Open Your Options

Just because you start a business with the intention of selling to a specific niche doesn't mean that you can't open up your options at some point. While you want to stay focused on this niche for your earliest stages in business, you should expect to expand into other niches as you continue to grow.

When you are evolving into other niches, think about things that your existing clients already like. Since individuals are usually multifaceted, you can try and identify one or two niches that your existing customer base likes in addition to the one you already serve. Then, you can expand into that niche. This gives you the benefit of already having an audience who would be interested in that niche, while also showing that you are a growing business and that you have the intention of meeting all of their retail needs.

If you think about any major company who has earned a large income through e-commerce you will notice that they started small but rapidly scaled by introducing new product lines and categories into their business. For example, Amazon.com started as an online book retailer and later expanded into being an online department store where you can purchase virtually anything you desire to purchase, no matter what the niche or product category is. If you want to grow large like Amazon.com, you need to think large like they do.

Intimately Know Who Your Customers Are

It is one thing to have an idea of who your target audience is, but as you are in business, you should have one primary goal: to know your customers intimately. The more intimately you know your customers, the better you will be able to serve them. When you can serve your customers in a way that is intimate to them, you end up being one of their favorite retailers and you earn customer loyalty.

While it is important to know who your entire audience is, you want to focus primarily on the *best* customers you have. The top 20% of your customers tend to drive 80% of your business, so knowing who these people are can increase your ability to serve them and maintain their loyalty. Take the time to really understand who they are, where they come from, why they shop with you, what needs you fulfill for them, and where your growth opportunities lie with these customers. The more you can serve them, the greater your business will grow.

Use Influential Customers to Acquire New Ones

As previously discussed, using influencers is a powerful way to increase your marketing potential and expand your audience. Influential customers have the potential to expose you to a greater market and provide you with social proof and social affirmation which is a large portion of what drives sales in online businesses.

Of your best customers, you can likely identify a few or even a segment of your customer market who has a major impact on whether or not people are going to buy from you. Your best customers likely advocate on your behalf and recommend you at any opportunity they get. Use these customers as an opportunity to expand your market. Let them know how much you appreciate their feedback and loyalty and show your appreciation. Perhaps you might consider giving them special perks or bonuses to encourage them to continue raving about your business and sending more business in your direction. If they are a major online influencer, you might even consider providing them with a unique code so that their followers can access special perks as well. Doing these types of activities can have a major impact in how rapidly your business will grow and how many new customers you can access.

Think of it this way, those who are already raving about your business are being positively impacted by your brand, products, and marketing strategies. Why not incorporate them into your existing strategies? The better you treat them, the longer they will remain your loyal fans. The longer they remain your loyal fans, the more they will tout about you to their friends and encourage their friends to shop with you. Their cheer and excitement will rub off and it is likely that some of their friends may become your loyal fans as well. As a result, you further increase the amount of leads you gain for new customers. It can truly pay off to treat your best customers like royalty when they are shopping with you.

Create a Memorable Brand

Brands that are memorable are brands that are frequently purchased from. Coca-Cola, Nike, Adidas, Eddie Bauer, Old Navy, Carters, Apple, Microsoft, Xbox and other memorable brands have all become common household names because their brands are distinct and memorable. There are thousands of other household brand names that are memorable as well, simply because they were effective in creating a brand that was memorable to their customers. If you can successfully create a memorable brand, you will be sure to stay relevant in people's minds.

Even if you don't shop from the aforementioned brands, it is likely that you know exactly who they are and what they sell. The same goes for many other brand names that you may hear or see on a regular basis. Effective branding strategies go a long way when it comes to creating a strong brand image and encouraging customer sales. When people can recognize your brand, they develop a type of relationship with it. As a result, you can increase the number of sales you get based off of your unique brand image.

Your brand image should be the same throughout every single thing that has to do with your business. Marketing strategies, social media profiles, content, websites, and anything else that has to do with your business should follow the branding image you have created. Fonts, colors, images, tones, personalities, and vocabulary should all stay consistent across every single thing that is related to your business in any way, shape, or form. This is how you can create a strong and consistent brand that can be recognized by anyone from anywhere, whether they will ever directly purchase from you or not. Remember, even if someone won't ever buy from you, it doesn't mean they will never refer you to someone who might.

Ask for Feedback

Every successful e-commerce site has some system for requesting feedback from qualified paying customers. Feedback from your customers is a large part of what will drive future sales.

In brick and mortar stores customers can discuss products with sales associates, physically inspect products, and assess for quality and desirability simply by being in the store. When you run an online business your customers rely on the feedback from others to drive the sales of future customers. People like to know that others who have already invested their money in your products have had a positive experience. Feedback can give information about quality, user friendliness, service experiences and more. Customers rely heavily on this to assist them with making future purchases.

In the beginning, it may be difficult to get feedback. If you need, you can purchase some products and give them away to friends and family so that they can physically test the item. Then, they can leave feedback on your website for you. Once they have done that, you will have the ball rolling for future sales. As more people purchase, you can request feedback and eventually, you will generate higher feedback volumes. The more positive feedback you get, the better sales you will have overall. However, it is important to remember that one bad review can have a major impact on the way people view your products. Even if you have hundreds of positive reviews, a couple of bad ones can lead people to believe that your product is hit-or-miss. Depending on the expenses related to your product, this could be the difference between making sales or not. As a result, you want to make sure that customers are made aware that if they have any issues with their experience they should first contact you or your support team so that you can rectify the issue. Then you have an opportunity to turn a negative into a positive before a negative review ever hits your page. In fact, you may even earn a positive review as a result.

Grow from The Inside

When you are expanding your business, you want to focus on growing from the inside as well as the outside. While attracting new customers and growing your sales is vital, you also want to make sure that your internal business operations are growing healthily, too. You can do this in several ways.

First, you want to make sure that you are using strong platforms and automation systems to run your business. The better your systems are, the more benefit you are going to gain from them and the higher quality your business will be. Make sure that you are never stingy when you are investing in systems for your business. If you have to stay cost-effective in the beginning, be sure to make it a priority to upgrade to the highest quality systems when you can afford to. Remember, highest quality doesn't always mean most expensive. There are many high-quality systems out there that are cost-effective as well.

In addition to your computerized systems, you need to consider your actual manual systems as well. How you are operating your business is important, you want to make sure that anything that is being manually operated is being done to the highest quality possible. As you grow, that will mean that you need to hire employees to assist you with the operations. Marketing assistants, social media managers, virtual assistants, customer support assistants and other employees can be an asset to your business as you continue to grow. The more you emphasize on customer experience, the more customers are going to want to work with your business. You should always make sure that when you are expanding rapidly on the outside, you are adjusting your expansion on the inside to adequately meet the needs of your growing business.

Growing your business is important. If you want to create a dropshipping empire that will earn you six figures, you need to be able to grow your business effectively. There are many factors that go into having a business that will grow in your favor. Your marketing strategies, order fulfillment strategies, customer support strategies, and other business-related strategies all need to be reinforced to ensure that your business is operating as efficiently as possible. The smoother your business operates, the greater you will be able to grow it. It is important to realize that in order for your business to grow, you can't be the only one running it. Investing in high-quality help is important, and you should prepare to do so as early as possible. Ideally, you want to invest in people who are already knowledgeable about e-commerce business, or the specific need you are hiring them for, such as marketing. By having experienced employees in your business, you can increase the amount of growth you experience over shorter periods of time. As a result, your business will evolve much more rapidly and you will be able to start earning a six-figure income even sooner.

Chapter 7: Marketing

Marketing your dropshipping business is a highly important aspect of keeping your business active and thriving. If there are any two areas you are going to invest in most, make it your website and your marketing. These are the areas that will work most towards the thriving of your company. Everything else can be focused on after these two aspects come together.

When you market your business effectively, you reach the eyes of several potential leads, including warm and hot leads who will actually end up purchasing from you. If you don't market, no one will know your business exists and so they won't be able to purchase anything from you. Marketing is an important element when it comes to creating a successful dropshipping business that will attract significant numbers of clients and earn you a six-figure income.

In previous chapters, we have touched base on some marketing tactics, but now you are going to learn how you can deploy an entire marketing plan so that your business grows rapidly. The following tactics should be meshed into place to create your overall marketing strategy. Each of these tasks is simple, generally cost effective, and can be put into place by anyone.

Social Proof Marketing

As you now know, social proof is a large part of what goes into making new customers purchase your products. If there are a series of positive reviews floating around about your business and your products, you are much more likely to make sales. Many people will even exit your website and do an external search about your business before they submit a sale. People want to make sure that they are investing their money into products that are high quality and that will meet or exceed their expectations, not low-quality products that will either break or end up in the back of the closet after a short amount of time.

There are many ways to integrate social proof marketing into your business. You can ask influencers to talk about you on their social media platforms, you can ask influencers or happy customers to make videos of their positive experiences and submit them to you, you can feature positive reviews on your social media platforms, and you can ask for word-of-mouth referrals from clients who have already purchased from you.

Influencer Engagement

When you are asking an influencer to talk about you on their social media platforms, they are going to want to have some of your products to test out. Ideally, you want to start them from the beginning of the customer experience that everyone experiences. Allow them to pick out 1-2 products that they like from your website and then give them a promo code so that they can purchase them for free. Have the orders fulfilled by the dropshipping method and request that the influencer honestly discusses your company and how they feel about your service. Then, they should also show the product off to their followers and discuss how they feel about the product.

If you want and can afford to, you might consider providing the influencer with a unique promo code that they can offer to their followers to earn a certain percentage off. This is called an affiliate link. Often, the affiliates will have some type of reward system for the number of customers who purchase through them. The most common system is to give them a small portion of product credit per customer who purchases through their affiliate link.

The benefit of using influencers this way is that people rely on hearing positive reviews from others. If you are tapping into influencers who already have a large following, you can likely assume that most of their following has established a trust in the influencer. Because of that trust, their followers will be more likely to purchase your products because someone they trust told them to. As a result, you can expect an increase in sales.

Influencer Video Marketing

For influencer video marketing you don't necessarily need influencers only for this marketing strategy. You can use virtually any happy customer who is willing to share their experience live. Once they do, you can share the video with your own followers and in targeted marketing campaigns and it will increase the number of sales you earn.

Influencer video marketing requires a few things to ensure that it actually works. First, you need to make sure that you have written consent from the client for publishing their video on your platforms. This will protect you in case of any legal events. Next, you want to ask that the customer uses a high-resolution video camera, films in a naturally lit area that is receiving adequate lighting and that they create a professional and attractive looking video. You should also ask that they give their honest experience with the products as they use them or review them live on camera for the first time. The best time for them to film is when they initially open the box when it arrives in the mail, but for some products like toothpaste or makeup, you may request that they film when they are actually using the products for the first time.

Once these customers submit their videos, you can pick the best ones and then begin your paid marketing campaigns with them. You can share them to your social media pages, boost those posts, and make unique paid advertisements for each of the videos. These videos are valuable because they allow customers to actually physically see the product in action. They can see people's reactions to the products and as a result, it may spark their interest towards the product even more. When people see products in action, they are much more likely to buy the product because they feel as though they know what to expect. It creates a more dynamic interface as opposed to simply using pictures on a website and attempting to encourage people that they are high-quality products.

Featuring Positive Reviews

Another great way to use social proof marketing is to feature positive reviews. If you gain access from the customer you can feature the review with their name attached. However, if you don't, you can simply use the words from the review and leave the reviewer's name out of it. Featuring positive reviews can help add to the tone of your website and social media pages. You can feature these on your sales pages, on your home page, or even on a special "testimony" page that customers can browse to in order to get an idea of how previous clients have enjoyed your work.

When you are a very young business, customers may rely on your testimonial page more than they will in the future. Since you are extremely young there will likely be no reviews floating around about your business because there is simply no one out there to review it and post it to their public communication boards. Once your business starts growing, however, you can expect that reviews will be posted on various other online platforms. Social media, blogs, streamed videos, and public forums are all areas where your business will likely be reviewed by people once it grows larger and more people begin purchasing from you. Emphasizing on the positive reviews can have a positive impact on your business and the amount of success you experience.

Word-Of-Mouth Referrals

Even though you are running an online retail store, word-of-mouth referrals are still important. When you have someone purchase products from you, you should ask them for any word-of-mouth referrals they may be willing to offer. You can do this by including it in an email they receive after they have made the purchase. For example, wait the expected shipping time plus a couple of days and then send an email that says something to the effect of "Hey, make sure to tell all of your friends how much you loved this product! Don't keep us a secret!"

Word-of-mouth referrals are still a reliable and solid version of social proof that encourages many people to purchase products. When people see positive reviews floating around, they will be more inclined to start looking at your products, but when people are actually told to purchase your products, they will be more likely to do so. When it comes to spending their money, people like to be *told* where the best places to spend it are. That way they can feel positive that they are spending it in a place that is worth their investment.

Social Media Marketing

Especially as an e-commerce business, social media marketing is going to be your gold mine. While you can use paid social media marketing, for this section we are only going to talk about unpaid social media marketing. There are many ways to use unpaid social media marketing to create a business that will increase your customer engagement and encourage sales.

Regular Posting

When you are working to advertise through social media, it is imperative that you post on a regular basis. Social media algorithms will end up hiding your stuff from your audience if you are not updating on a regular basis. They keep active and relevant pages that have a high customer engagement in front of the audience and let everyone else fall to the back. It is important that you understand this and post on a regular basis to ensure that you are staying at the forefront of the newsfeeds of your customers and are reaching them on a regular basis. Plus, the more they see your company name, the more likely they are going to inquire about your business. Research shows that it takes 7-14 times for someone to see your business name before they will even open your website and take a look at what you have to offer. From there, it may take another 7-14 time for them to actually invest their money with you. Make sure that you are posting regularly so that you can reach these numbers with hundreds and thousands of unique people.

Informative and Entertaining Posts

There are many different types of content you can post, but the most commonly posted content should be informative and entertaining. If your entire page is covered in call-to-action posts, no one will pay attention to you because your page simply looks like a giant advertisement. Instead, provide informative and entertaining posts that can teach people about your business and give them something fun to keep them captivated. When you do this, they will be more likely to scroll your page. You can establish a positive feeling in them which will make them feel happy and inquisitive when they reach your call-to-action posts which will be scattered throughout. This means that they will be much more likely to say "yes" to the post and look into it further. The goal is to keep potential customers coming back to your page and keep them on your page for more than a few seconds at a time. These posts should make up about 80% of your entire posting feed. If you want to, you may consider drawing the posts out to your business website where you share blog posts and then the blog posts lead to specific sales pages for certain products. This is called having a sales funnel.

Call-To-Action Posts

The other 20% of your posts should be call-to-action posts. These are posts that are clearly advertising products, promotions, or your business altogether. They should be posted much less frequently than the informative and entertaining posts, but they still need to be posted. These are an important tool that can draw people to your page and encourage them to buy from you. If you aren't updating your call-to-action posts regularly enough, people may land on your page and fail to realize that your page is linked to an actual retail company. As a result, you lose out on potential traffic and your business will slow down.

Paid Advertisements

Another effective method of marketing is paid advertisements. As much as you may want to shy away from these methods, you want to make sure that you are actively using them. Spending money on your marketing is one of the most effective and efficient ways to push your business in front of people who may not otherwise see your business. You can choose a certain audience and have your ads target these people. As a result, your ad will reach people who you otherwise have zero contact with.

There are many platforms that offer paid advertising. Virtually every single social media platform offers paid advertising. You can also use Google Adwords, Amazon.com, and other larger paid advertising platforms as well. These platforms are excellent for allowing you to reach your audience more rapidly and expand your business quicker as a result.

Before you invest in paid advertising make sure that you understand what goes into a paid advertisement. Many people do not realize that there is a certain structure that needs to take place in order to get people to actually click on your ads. If your ad is not made up properly people will simply overlook it. Your ad needs to be captivating and strike curiosity in order to gain traction with your target audience. Otherwise, people will overlook it as "just another product for sale". You need to make people realize that they *need* your product within' a matter of seconds through a single image/text combination. It is important that you do your research to find out how this works with your unique audience.

Promotions

Especially in the beginning, having effective promotions in place can encourage sales. People love seeing that they will save money on your products, and this is especially true when there are no existing reviews on the products themselves. The less they have to spend on the product, the more likely they are going to buy it. The sweet-spot for these purchases is between $10-$50. At this point, people are more willing to gamble their money without doing extensive research on how others' have enjoyed the product. Below $10 and it becomes too cheap for them to purchase as taxes and shipping will make it unreasonable, and over $50 it becomes too expensive to gamble their money on.

When you have a promotion ongoing with your business,a you will want to market it using paid advertising as well as your social media platforms and website pages. Make sure that you push the promotion into as many different areas of your marketing strategy as possible so that it is viewed by as many people as it can be. This will ensure that it is seen and that people take advantage of the promotion. If you promote it through paid advertisements, but your social media pages and website don't reflect the change, people will likely think it's a scam and will not have trust in your business.

Email Marketing

Although many promotional emails end up in the trash folder, they are still a highly effective marketing strategy. The simple act of seeing your business name appear in their email on a regular basis can keep your company relevant in their minds which can prompt them to purchase from you. If your subject lines are strong enough, people will want to inquire about what you are selling. For example, if they see your name 7 different times in their inbox and finally on the 8th time they see it and it says "25% off" they are likely going to take a look just to see what you have available at that time. This will lead to them making further purchases.

Even though your e-mails may not be opened and viewed as often, it is important that you are still keeping the content relevant and interesting. You never know when someone is going to open up your email and start browsing through to see what you have available. There are many templates out there for effective email marketing campaigns if you are inexperienced with this process. You can also use automated systems like MailChimp or Ontraport to automate your emails to your customers.

Marketing is one of the most important aspects of your entire business. You need to have strong marketing campaigns in place if you are ever going to reach your customers. If there are two areas you put your main focus on in your business, aside from customers, let it be your retail website and your marketing strategies. These are the two areas that are going to serve your customer the most and attract them to your website so that they can experience the business you have designed just for them.

Chapter 8: Common Mistakes

There are many common mistakes that prevail in the dropshipping industry. While these mistakes are honest and simple, they have the ability to totally wreck your business. In this chapter, we are going to explore what these common mistakes are, how they can affect your business, and how you can avoid them in your own business.

Shipping Rates

In the dropshipping business, you are going to be exposed to many different shipping rates. Vendors charge differently and the rates can range all over the board. Many suppliers will try and compensate and end up charging obscene amounts for shipping, or they simply don't charge enough. It can be tough to estimate what shipping is going to cost for various orders, especially when they are being ordered from a number of different vendors. If you charge too much you may drive customers away, and if you charge too little you will end up eating into your own profits. The best thing to do is to find the average shipping charges between the vendors you are actively using and charge flat rate shipping. You may choose to have different divisions for shipping, for example, orders under $100 may have one rate while orders over have another. This makes it easier for you to get enough money to cover shipping without eating into your profits. While some customers may end up slightly over paying for shipping, others will underpay so it ends up evening out for you as the retailer.

Relying on Vendors Too Much

Of course, dropshippers need to rely on their vendors as these are the people who are supplying your products for you, but there is a point where you need to be able to stop relying on them. To put it simply, you do not want to put all of your eggs in one basket.

When you rely too much on one vendor you run into a high number of issues in your business. You might run into issues where there is inadequate stock to fill your orders and due to a lack of backups, you do not have any alternatives for you to fulfill order requirements. Or, you may run into an issue where the entire vendor is down for a few days, or longer, and therefore your entire business is negatively affected. Relying too heavily on one vendor is not ideal. That is why when you were going through the getting started process,cl you were prompted to pick at least two vendors to start with. Over time you will want to expand this more. For each new product line, you should have at least two vendors who can supply your products for you. This will keep you from running out and having to issue refunds or inform paying customers that their orders will be delayed and you will not be able to honor your promised shipping rates and times.

Expecting it to Be Too Easy

While dropshipping is a relatively simple business that can be automated to provide you with a passive income stream, it doesn't mean that you won't have to do any work to earn your income stream. You need to be prepared to put in the work in order to see your business grow. Setting up your business is the hardest part, this will take the most of your time and effort as you want to make sure everything is in place. Once your business is completely set up, the management process is significantly easier.

If you have the resources, you might consider hiring some help right out of the gate. While this may be a little preemptive, having people on board who are experienced with business launches can significantly increase your growth rates and make it easier for you to expand at the rate you desire to expand at.

This business is certainly an easier one to get into, but it does still require you to put in work. Do not think that you can simply slap together a couple of things and have a totally functional six-figure business. You will need to put in the work to build your business if you are going to earn the profit you desire. However, once your business is established and you are able to hire help, it will become an extremely passive income stream that requires little to none of your own attention.

Not Enough Branding Display

When you are running a dropshipping company, your brand is not attached to products. While other companies have their brands and logos displayed all over products, your products will display other people's logos or none at all. As a result, you need to ensure that you have your brand displayed adequately in all other areas of your business. Your website, social media pages, emails and anything else that allows you to interact with the customer should have your brand on it. All of your marketing campaigns should have your brand as well. It is important that you do your best to market your brand as effectively as possible. That way people will remember who you are, even though their products don't have your brand name on them.

Difficult to Access Order Information

When a customer orders an item from you, they want to be able to identify where their order is and when they can expect to get it. Many dropshippers do not consider this aspect and fail to make the order information easily accessible. For an enhanced customer service experience, you should make this information accessible to every single customer who purchases through you. You can do this easily by having automated emails that send out information regarding the shipment. Allow the email to include information such as the order number, when the order was purchased, the purchase price, what is included in the order, and when the order is expected to arrive. You should also provide easy to use instructions for what customers can do if they are unhappy with their order or if they experience any issues with the shipping process.

Not Enough Emphasis on The Customer

Because of how automated the dropshipping business is, it can be easy to forget how important your customer is to your business success. Many dropshipping companies fail to recognize the importance of their customers and therefore end up accidentally creating a customer experience that is undesirable and difficult. As a result, they may end up losing a significant number of potential leads and gaining negative feedback from customers who did go through and purchase products from the company.

Even though there are many important aspects of your business, such as your website and marketing tactics, your customer is always the most important part. If you are not emphasizing on your customer you will end up creating a business that does not serve their needs and therefore you will have a business that fails. A business that does not attract clients is a business that does not earn income. Remember that.

There are many mistakes that new business owners make, and it is completely normal. Dropshipping companies feature a significant amount of automation and therefore they can make it even easier for you to run into mistakes that you didn't even think of. You should think of your retail store like a machine. Each part of the machine needs to operate efficiently if you are going to have a business that effectively serves your target market and earns you a six-figure income. Make sure that you recognize these mistakes and set yourself up to avoid being affected by them in your own business so that you don't face the potentially lethal side effects that they can have on your success.

Chapter 9: Exit Strategies

Every business, even an e-commerce business, needs a solid exit strategy. There are two reasons why you would need to use your exit strategy: either you are not earning enough, or you do not want to keep the business and therefore you want to sell it. Regardless of your reason, having a strong exit strategy in place will ensure that you are prepared for when that time comes.

Exit strategies are simple to create and should be reviewed regularly. Make sure that you are well aware of the terms that surround your exit strategy so that you can be prepared for when your business hits the point where you are ready to make an exit. While it may not come for many years, maybe not even in your lifetime if you choose to pass the business down, having the exit strategy in place and regularly reviewing it is important.

Close Down or Sell

If you are running a business that is not thriving, it may be time to deploy an exit strategy that allows you to shut down your business. While in some cases you can simply shut down shop, in others you may still need to have orders fulfilled and inform existing customers of your impending close. Make sure that you are closing down shop effectively if you are going to do so. You never want to leave your customers hanging because this can lead to you having a difficult time launching a new business and gaining trust in the future. Yes, just because you close down one store does not mean you can't open up a new one in the future.

If you are running a business that is successful or better yet, thriving, then you will want to consider selling your business. This way, you don't take a loss or simply have the income stop flowing. Instead, you can sell your business to someone else who desires to keep it running and you can earn a profit from the effort you put into building your business and getting it to the level where it is now. If you want to sell your business as an exit strategy, it could be because you are not interested in staying in business, because you are looking to make a change in career, because this was the plan all along, or because it has reached a point where you are no longer interested in keeping it going. Regardless of what your own reason will be, you should do your best to identify it early on and create a strategy around that plan.

Business Appraisals

Before you sell your business,ch you need to appraise it. There are many things that go into the appraisal of your business. You may want to consider hiring a professional appraiser to help you with this process as they will be able to give you the most accurate value of your business. The appraisal is more than just knowing how much gross revenue and profit you earn from your business each year. It also factors in the amount of potential growth that can be expected and the strength of the foundation upon which the business was built on.

Before you sell your business, you will always want to appraise it. This will allow you to know what your value is worth. Knowing the true worth of your business means that you can negotiate more effectively and accept offers that are actually reasonable to the value of your business. If you don't know this number, you shouldn't be selling your business just yet.

The Selling Process

Selling a business can be difficult. Just because the business has a certain value does not mean that you are going to get that value from a potential buyer. In fact, you may not get any offers for the first while. In other cases, you may sell the business almost immediately for asking price. For your best interest, you should go into the process with the expectations that you are going to have to be patient and wait for a seller. This keeps you from having to rush and jump on any low baller offer that is tossed your way.

Many people are looking for "turn-key" businesses or businesses which they can buy and maintain as they already are and simply earn the profit from. They do not want to have to invest a significant amount of work into earning their profit, at least not initially. They simply want to step into the driver's seat and expand their business as rapidly as possible without having to put any work into the foundation. The more established your business already is, the more opportunity you will have to sell it to potential buyers.

You should be prepared to negotiate with your potential buyers. There is a good chance that they will come to you with a low offer. If they do, you need to know what the value of your business is and know what you are willing to settle for at your lowest amount. Still, you want to negotiate to bring their number up to as close to the valuation as possible. The more valuable your business is, the more negotiation will need to happen as this is when more complex deals come into play.

Something that most businesses offer which you should be prepared to offer as well is a limited amount of ongoing support. You should be prepared to offer the buyer at least 30 days of support with email systems and guidance so that they can learn to seamlessly take over the company. This gives them the opportunity to have a smoother take over instead of them stepping in and not being clear on how you have run your company until this point. It also assists with the sale process as people like knowing that they will be guided to take over your success instead of plopped into the seat of a car they don't know how to drive.

Remember, just because you reach the negotiation process with a certain potential buyer doesn't mean you are going to make a sale. You might negotiate with many potential buyers before you reach a deal that actually meets your needs for your business. Don't feel obligated to make a sale just because you have entered the negotiation phase with a potential buyer. In fact, reaching this stage and leaving it if the clauses aren't promising for yourself as the seller can work in your favor. In some cases, when a buyer is particularly motivated, threatening to reject the deal altogether can encourage them to come closer to your desired value. It shows them that you have decided what you want for the business and that you are not willing to sell for any less. It also shows that your company is actually valuable because you aren't willing to sell it off for any ballpark number.

When to Sell?

As aforementioned, you will likely have your own reason as to why you are going in business. If you are going into business with the intention to build a six figure business, you likely want to keep your business running until you no longer desire to run it. However, you may also want to sell it when it reaches a certain valuation so that you can walk away with a lump sum from the business.

When you decide to sell your business will largely depend on what your intention with the business is. Once you have decided what will trigger the sale, then you need to pick the perfect time to actually get into the market and sell your business.

The first thing you need to consider is the state of your business. A company that is on an upward trend for gaining profit and traffic is one that will have greater sales potential and a higher valuation. People want a business that is growing, not one that has reached its peak or is beginning to dwindle. When your business is in a state of thriving, it is a good time to consider entering the market for the sale of your business.

Another thing to consider is the state of the current market. While businesses will almost always sell well, a recessed market may result in you having to settle for less than your business is worth just to make the sale. If you are not willing to take the hit on your sale price you will want to wait until the economy comes back up so that you can earn your desired value from your business.

Once your business and the market are in the right position, you can consider selling your business off. This will provide you with the opportunity to earn a large amount of capital off of it which you can invest elsewhere. With that money, you may consider starting a new business venture or investing in one that you are already operating so that you can grow it significantly. That is completely up to you.

Having a strong exit strategy in place for your business is extremely important. Any business, even one that is anticipated to stay in business for a long period of time, needs to have an exit strategy. There are many reasons as to why you may want to exit your business and having this strategy in place can give you the opportunity to make an efficient exit that will not damage your success or profits. Make sure that when you are in the process of creating your business plan that you also create an effective exit strategy that will allow you to exit the market properly when you are ready to. An improper exit strategy can lead to you selling prematurely, losing money, or otherwise running into a rookie mistake with your exit strategy.

Chapter 10: Tips and Tricks

As you begin working your dropshipping business, you are going to begin to learn your own tips and tricks to help you master the business. However, to help you get started, we have compiled a list of some of the best tips and tricks you should pay attention to when you are starting your dropshipping business. Having this knowledge under your belt now and applying them immediately will ensure that you are prepared for everything that is to come and that you come out of the gates strong.

It is a good idea to keep a book handy so that as you learn your own tips and tricks in the industry, you can write them down. While you may remember some due to using them on a regular basis, having them written down can help you remember what works in the situations you don't tend to experience as often, such as specific situations with certain vendors. Make sure that you keep this notebook handy and that you use it whenever you need in order to make sure that you are running your business smoothly and efficiently.

Reputation

As with any business, your reputation is highly important. You need to recognize what goes into creating a solid reputation and how you can use your reputation to positively impact your business performance. Your reputation is closely attached to your brand, but it is not your brand itself. Instead, it is the way people think about your brand.

Take a moment to think about a company that you haven't had such a good experience with. It is likely that many people haven't had a good experience, and for you and the rest of the population, their reputation is tarnished. People may continue to shop there, but it does not equate to them gaining as much business as they could if they had a positive reputation.

Now, think about a business that you love shopping with. Think about how positive they make you feel and the type of experience you have when you do business with them. Also, think about how other people tend to talk about that business. Since their overall reputation is more positive and they are known to serve their customers effectively, it is likely that their reputation is excellent.

With your own business, you want to be the one with the reputation that has people eager to work with you. People should be aware of how positive your business is and the type of experience they can expect to have with you well before the first time they ever do business with you. When people run into issues with their service, they should be able to rely on the fact that your company will rectify the situation quickly and in a justified manner. The customer needs to know that you are always going to look out for their best interest and do everything you can to serve them to the highest of your abilities.

Clear Communication

Many dropshippers fail to notify their customers about the nature of their business. Customers are led to believe that the retailer holds all of the supplies and that they are independently responsible for all inventory-related operations when in reality they are not. This can lead to miscommunication with the customer and can create a lack of trust in the business. It is important that you are always clear and up front with your customers that they are purchasing from a dropshipping retailer and that you do not have any involvement with the inventory that your store stocks.

When you do this, you maintain a transparency with your customers that earns their trust. You also relieve some of the pressure from your own business in the event that something goes wrong. When people are aware that you work with dropship suppliers, they gain the ability to realize that some troubles may be experienced that will take you slightly longer to rectify due to the outsourced suppliers. It gives you the opportunity to have some slack from your customers.

Tracking Numbers

It is extremely important that you obtain tracking numbers from your suppliers whenever they ship products for your customers. Make sure that all of your suppliers offer tracking numbers and that you utilize them with your shipping process. Tracking numbers are important for protecting not only yourself but your customer as well.

When you get tracking numbers, it adds a level of convenience to the system for your suppliers. It also adds security for you and your business. Since you will be able to track the products as they are being shipped, you will be able to tell where they may have gotten lost if that happens, or if the order has been delivered but someone claims it hasn't been. It is important that you have tracking numbers associated with every single shipment.

Delivery Time

When you are working on getting suppliers, it is vital that you understand what their delivery time is. Various companies will have different shipping lengths so try and find an average length and then look for companies who can work within' this average. Then, you can also provide this average on your website. When you are letting people know approximately how long shipping takes, always be sure to under promise and over deliver. What that means is: if the average shipping time with your suppliers is 7 to 14 days, tell your customers it will be 12 to 17 days. That way if the product arrives in less than 7 days they will be pleasantly surprised, but if it goes into the longer shipping times, your customer won't feel as though they have been lied to about shipping periods.

Warranties

Depending on what value your products are, you may want to consider offering a warranty for your products. Offering warranties on high valued items can make it easier for you to sell the item because people feel as though their investment has been protected. It also shows that you are committed to customer satisfaction.

How you choose to construct your warranty will be entirely up to you. You want to make sure that your warranty will protect your customer without it costing you a large amount of money. Because of this you also want to make sure that your suppliers are providing you with high-quality products that won't be likely to break down. Having a proper warranty in place is important if you are going to provide one, so take some time to research what similar warranties look like and how they are constructed for the customer and the business so you can get an idea of how your own warranty should look. Make sure you advertise the warranty on the product page as it is a great selling point for many products, especially those that are high value.

Samples

Before you commit to using any dropshipping company you always want to make sure that you are testing out samples of their products first. Any good quality dropshipping supplier will allow you to purchase a couple of samples of their products so that you can test the quality of their products. It allows you to see if you like what they have to offer and if it reflects the type of quality you want to provide for your customers.

If a company does not allow you to purchase samples from them, you can almost always find an alternative that will allow you to. If you absolutely must go through a specific company, you might consider purchasing one of their units from a company that already dropships their products. While you will pay an inflated fee for the sample, it will allow you to test out the product and see what you think of the quality and value it offers to your own customers.

Modest Start

When you are starting a new company you always want to start modestly. No matter how much research you conduct before starting your company, nothing will ever compare to hands-on experience. Allowing yourself to start modestly will give you the opportunity to learn everything along the way and develop a strong understanding of your business so that when you expand you are prepared to handle the developments and you are clear on your role in the business.

Learning these tips and tricks before you officially kick off your business will help you start ahead of the game. While you will still need hands-on experience to make sure that you master your own business, being able to have this knowledge in mind beforehand will set you up for success in the long run. Make sure that you keep a notebook on hand so you can jot down your own lessons along the way so that you are always prepared for each situation and you can refer back to your notes in difficult situations.

Conclusion

Starting a dropshipping business is an incredible way to earn yourself a six-figure income. There are many ways to start a dropshipping business, but this streamlined guide will allow you to start one efficiently and reach your six-figure income as quickly as possible. Even though dropshipping is a passive income stream, you should be prepared to put in a fair amount of work to establish your business beforehand. Once you establish your business and have regular sales going through your website, you can seek to hire assistants which can allow you to further remove yourself from the business making it an even more passive income source.

I hope that this book was able to clearly guide you through the process of starting your own dropshipping business. Each chapter was designed to be a clear and concise guide walking you through each step of the business so that you can start with a strong plan. By following this guide you will certainly be able to start your own business that will have the potential to earn you a six-figure income.

The next step is for you to start putting these plans into action. If you haven't been working step-by-step through the book, then it is time to go back to the beginning and start implementing the strategies from this book into the development of your dropshipping business. Make sure that you pay close attention to the common mistakes and tips and tricks that have been outlined in this book as they will provide you with the knowledge you need to strategize a strong start in your dropshipping business. That way you can ensure that you set yourself up for total success.

Lastly, if you enjoyed this book, I ask that you please take the time to rate it on Amazon Kindle. Your honest review would be greatly appreciated.

Thank you, and best of luck in creating your six-figure dropshipping business.

www.ingramcontent.com/pod-product-compliance
Lightning Source LLC
Chambersburg PA
CBHW071255170526
45165CB00003B/1349